Native Americans

The Cheyenne

Richard M. Gaines

ABDO Publishing Company

Published by ABDO Publishing Company, 4940 Viking Drive, Suite 622, Edina, Minnesota 55435. Copyright © 2000 Abdo Consulting Group, Inc., Pentagon Tower, P.O. Box 36036, Minneapolis, Minnesota 55435 USA. International copyrights reserved in all countries. No part of this book may be reproduced in any form without written permission from the publisher.

Published 2000
Printed in the United States of America
Second Printing 2002

Illustrator: David Fadden (pgs. 6, 7, 9, 10, 11, 13, 14, 17, 19, 21, 23)
Cover Photo: Corbis
Interior Photos: Corbis (pgs. 25, 27, 28, 29, 30)
Editors: Bob Italia, Tamara L. Britton, Kate A. Furlong
Art Direction & Maps: Pat Laurel
Border Design: Carey Molter/MacLean & Tuminelly (Mpls.)

Library of Congress Cataloging-in-Publication Data

Gaines, Richard M., 1942-
    The Cheyenne / Richard M. Gaines.
       p. cm. -- (Native Americans)
    Includes bibliographical references and index.
    Summary: Presents a brief introduction to the Cheyenne Indians including information on their society, homes, food, clothing, crafts, and life today.
    ISBN 1-57765-378-5
    1. Cheyenne Indians--Juvenile literature. [1. Cheyenne Indians. 2. Indians of North America--Montana.] I. Title.

E99.C53 G35 2000
978'.004973--dc21
                                                                99-059866

Contributing Editor: Barbara Gray, JD

Barbara Gray, JD (Kanatiyosh) is a member of the Mohawk Nation (Akwesasne), which is in New York State and Canada. Barbara earned her Juris Doctorate from Arizona State University College of Law in May of 1999. She is presently pursuing a Doctorate in Justice Studies that focuses on American Indian culture and issues at Arizona State University. When she finishes school, she will return home to the Mohawk Nation.

Illustrator: David Kanietakeron Fadden

David Kanietakeron Fadden is a member of the Akwesasne Mohawk Wolf Clan. His work has appeared in publications such as *Akwesasne Notes, Indian Time*, and the *Northeast Indian Quarterly*. Examples of his work have also appeared in various publications of the Six Nations Indian Museum in Onchiota, NY. His work has also appeared in "How The West Was Lost: Always The Enemy," produced by Gannett Production which appeared on the Discovery Channel. David's work has been exhibited in Albany, NY; the Lake Placid Center for the Arts; Centre Strathearn in Montreal, Quebec; North Country Community College in Saranac Lake, NY; Paul Smiths College in Paul Smiths, NY; and at the Unison Arts & Learning Center in New Paltz, NY.

Contents

Where They Lived

The Cheyenne call themselves Tsetschestahase (jis-jis-tus). They originally lived in earthen homes north of the Missouri River in present-day Minnesota. They were fishermen and farmers. Their language is part of the **Algonquian** language family.

The Cheyenne acquired the horse from the Kiowa around 1770. The horses allowed them to hunt the millions of buffalo that roamed the prairie. Soon after, the Cheyenne left their homes. They separated into northern and southern groups, and moved westward into the Great Plains.

The Northern Cheyenne went to present-day Montana and Wyoming. The Southern Cheyenne went into present-day Oklahoma and Colorado.

The Great Plains were mostly grassland. Trees grew near the rivers and streams that flowed from the Rocky Mountains. Other Native American tribes lived there, too. Often, these tribes did not get along. They would make war against the Cheyenne.

Long ago, the Cheyenne moved from Minnesota across the Great Plains, splitting into two groups. Today, the Northern Cheyenne live in Montana. The Southern Cheyenne live in Oklahoma.

Society

For most of the year, the Cheyenne lived in small bands of related families. Several times a year, the Northern and Southern tribes gathered for religious and seasonal festivals.

During these special gatherings, tipis were arranged in a giant circle, three or four deep. The east end of the circle was left open to greet the morning sun. Sometimes, there were a thousand tipis in the circle. It was a chance to camp with old friends and relatives.

In the center of the circle were two tipis. They were the religious centers. There, the tribe kept the "sacred bundles" of the Medicine Hat Lodge and the Medicine Arrow Lodge.

The Sacred Buffalo Hat bundle and the four Sacred Arrows

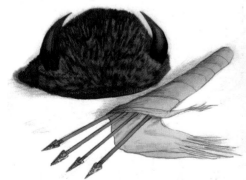

The Northern Cheyenne are the keepers of the Sacred Buffalo Hat bundle. The Sacred Buffalo Hat bundle contains the horned scalp of a female buffalo. The scalp is worn by the keeper of the Sacred Buffalo Hat bundle.

The Sacred Buffalo Hat was given to **Erect Horns** by the Creator. The Cheyenne believe that the Sacred Buffalo Hat possesses spiritual powers.

The Southern Cheyenne are the keepers of the four Sacred Arrows. They are kept in the Medicine Arrow Lodge. These four arrows were given to the Cheyenne **prophet**, Sweet Water. The Creator gave Sweet Water the arrows, the traditional teachings, and the prophecies to help the Cheyenne survive.

The Cheyenne also had six military societies. Any man of any age could join a military society. The societies were the Elk Soldiers, Fox Soldiers, Dog Soldiers, Shields Soldiers, Bowstrings, and the Northern Crazy Dogs.

The Dog Soldiers had much authority. They protected the people like police officers do today. They also camped together in the tipi circle.

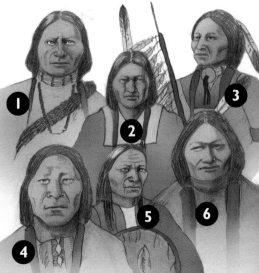

Members of the Cheyenne military societies:
1. Elk Soldiers 2. Shields Soldiers
3. Dog Soldiers 4. Bowstrings
5. Northern Crazy Dogs 6. Fox Soldiers

Homes

The Cheyenne lived in earthen, domed homes before they moved to the Great Plains. Then, they began to live in tipis. The tipi was a good home for the **nomadic** Cheyenne. That's because it was easy to move and set up.

The Cheyenne fitted their horses with a **travois**. It carried heavy loads, including the tipi.

When the Cheyenne reached a new campsite, the women quickly set up their tipi. They drew a circle on the ground. Then, they put up three long cedar or pine poles to make a triangle. These three poles were placed at the north, south, and east points of the circle. Then, they were tied together near the top.

Twelve more poles were placed around the circle. These poles were tied to the frame near the top. The poles were then tied to stakes with rope. Rope was made from braided hair taken from the top of a buffalo's head.

The tipi cover was made of summer buffalo hides sewn together by the women. The cover was wrapped around the outside of the pole frame. Then, it was fastened together at the front of the tipi with willow-wood pins. An opening at the bottom served as an entrance. A **tanned** buffalo hide was hung in front of the opening to create a door.

Inside the tipi, a three-foot-high (one-meter-high) liner was attached to the poles. The liner **insulated** the tipi. A fire was built in the tipi's center. This fire warmed the tipi and made it glow like a lantern.

The parts of a tipi: 1. Main pole frame 2. Outer pole frame 3. Sewn buffalo hide cover 4. Finished tipi with a buffalo hide door (5) and smoke flap (6).

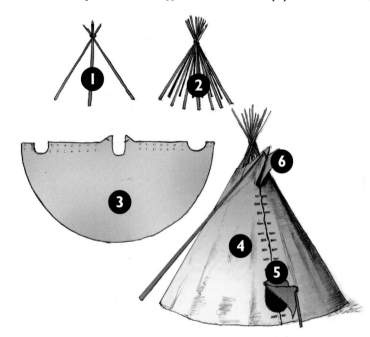

Food

When they lived in present-day Minnesota, the Cheyenne planted corn, squash, pumpkins, beans, and tobacco. The men fished. They also hunted duck, other marsh animals, and forest game.

The Cheyenne gathered wild rice from the marshes. They also picked fruits and berries. Women dug plant roots for stews and grilling. With plenty of game, fruits, and crops, the Cheyenne flourished.

Hunting buffalo

When they moved to the Great Plains, the Cheyenne stopped planting crops, except tobacco. So, the Cheyenne depended on buffalo for food.

The Cheyenne also traded with other Native American tribes and Europeans. They traded buffalo hides for corn, tobacco, coffee, and guns.

Cheyenne trading with a European

Clothing

Cheyenne men wore fringed shirts, breechcloths, and leggings made from tanned deer or elk hide. They also wore arm bands, head bands, and hung pipe bags and pouches from their waists.

In warm weather, the men often wore a breechcloth. In cooler weather, they wore decorated fringed shirts and deerskin leggings that tied in the front. Everyone wore robes of tanned deer, elk, or buffalo hides.

Before going into battle, men dyed their hair red. They also painted their faces in designs of blue, yellow, white, and black.

Cheyenne women wore dresses throughout the seasons. The dresses were made from brain-tanned deer or elk hide. The arm openings and the bottom hem of the dress were fringed. In cooler weather, women wore leggings.

Women wore leather belts around their waists. A leather bag was often hung from the belt. It held important tools like sewing needles. Sometimes, women wore a small leather pouch around their neck.

Men and women wore moccasins decorated with porcupine quills. In the 1800's, glass beads became a trade item. Women began using them instead of the quills.

Men and women also wore earrings made of bone or feather. The men wore necklaces made from **talons** or bear claws. Men and women wore quilled necklaces.

A Cheyenne family in traditional dress

Crafts

Cheyenne women made clothes from buffalo, deer, and elk hides. They scraped the fat and meat from the inside of the hide using a flesh tool. They cut the hair from the outside with a draw blade.

Women's Quilling Society

Hides were **tanned** with buffalo brains. The brains were cooked until oil floated to the top. Then, the brains and oil were rubbed into the hide, which preserved it.

To make the hide soft, the women pulled it through the hole in a buffalo shoulder bone. Once the hide was soft, it was cut, sewn, and decorated to make warm boots, skirts, and shirts.

The Cheyenne had a Women's Quilling Society. Its members made tipis, dresses, leggings, pouches, and shirts. Each member was responsible for quilling a certain item. The members passed on their knowledge and skills to the young women who joined the society.

Older women invited younger women to join the Quilling Society. There, the older women taught the younger women how to quill.

Porcupine quills were collected and cleaned. Then, the quills were dyed using natural plants and walnut hulls. The Cheyenne women made the quills flexible with saliva. Quills were gently pulled between the teeth to flatten them. Then they were used to create designs.

Quilling took much time and patience. The women used this time to share stories. This helped pass on tribal history and knowledge.

In the 1800's, traders brought glass seed beads to the Cheyenne. The beads made decorating faster and easier. But, special items were still made with quills.

Family

Before daybreak, the young men rose to feed the horses. Next, the grandmothers and mothers awoke to begin the daily breakfast. Everyone else rose when they wanted.

Breakfast was simple. Everyone ate when and what they wanted.

Each family member had daily tasks. But there was always time for play and talk among friends.

When a Cheyenne couple married, they moved into their own tipi. It was placed near the bride's mother's tipi. The groom gave meat to his mother-in-law. She gave some to all of her daughters' families who also lived nearby.

The daughters' children lived together near the grandmother's tipi. They called each other brother and sister.

Young men feeding horses at dawn

Children

Cheyenne children played many games. Some were just for fun. Others prepared the children for their adult roles.

The girls played with dolls and **cradleboards**. This got them ready to be mothers. The boys played hunting and **raiding** games. Sometimes, boys tried be the first to take meat off a drying frame without being seen. This game prepared them for capturing horses, hunting, and **counting coup**.

Thirteen- or fourteen-year-old boys were allowed to join their relatives' war parties. But they were not expected to fight. Instead, they worked as helpers and held horses. Girls learned their tasks and crafts from their mothers, grandmothers, and aunts.

After dark, fires lighted the tipis. The adults gathered around the fires and sang songs. Or they listened to the elders tell **legends** and adventure stories. These stories taught and entertained.

Children played in small groups outside in the dark. Or, they visited with other children in nearby tipis until they grew tired. Cheyenne children had no regular bedtimes.

By midnight, nearly everyone was asleep. The grandmothers covered the fires with dirt before they went to sleep.

Cheyenne girls playing with dolls on cradleboards

Myths

The Creator came to **Erect Horns** and gave him the **traditional** teachings and the Sacred Buffalo Hat.

One day, all the buffalo herds disappeared from the Great Plains. The Cheyenne began to starve. The tribal leaders chose Erect Horns and his wife to go on a **vision quest** and bring the buffalo back.

Erect Horns and his wife traveled westward for many days. Finally, they found a hollow, magic mountain. They entered the magic mountain during a lightning storm. There, they learned a dance and a prayer ceremony.

Erect Horns and his wife returned to the Cheyenne camp. They showed the tribe how to make a Medicine Dance Lodge that looked like the inside of the magic mountain. They taught the tribe the dance and prayer ceremony.

They showed the people the Sacred Buffalo Hat. They believed it had **supernatural** powers. The Creator told the Cheyenne to follow the **traditional** teachings, perform the prayers and dances, and the buffalo would return.

The Cheyenne used myths to explain many things about life. The story of Tomsivsi, or Erect Horns, explains how the Sacred Buffalo Hat ceremony made the buffalo and other animals plentiful so that the Cheyenne would not starve.

War

The Cheyenne went to war against other tribes to protect their territory. After the Europeans brought horses to America, Cheyenne war parties also **raided** enemy villages for food, horses, and supplies.

Any man could head a war party. First, he invited other men to a feast. There, he told them his battle plan. If the men agreed to go, they smoked a pipe that was passed around. If they did not want to go, they passed the pipe.

Before going to battle, the war party asked a medicine man to give them advice. He asked the spirits to make the war a success.

After a successful battle, the war party dressed in their finest war costumes. Then, they returned to the camp, shouting and displaying all the things they had captured. Everyone ran out to see the victory parade.

Not all war parties with other Great Plains tribes used violence. Cheyenne warriors also **counted coup**. Each scored a victory by touching the enemy without killing him, then returning safely to the camp.

Cheyenne weapons: 1. Arrow 2. Quiver 3. Bow
4. War Club 5. Shield 6. Tomahawk 7. Hatchet

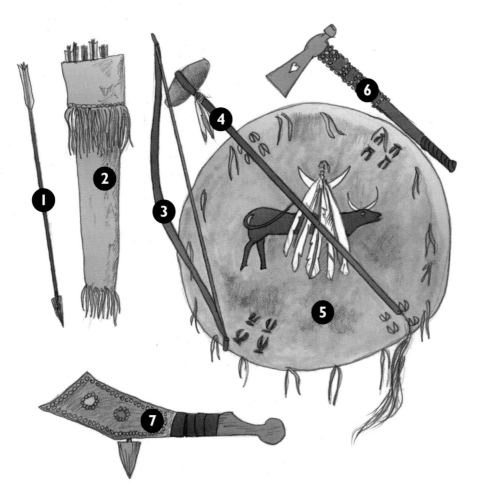

Contact with Europeans

In 1680, French explorer Sieur de La Salle built a fort on the Illinois River near present-day Peoria, Illinois. On February 24, a party of Cheyenne arrived. They had traveled more than 300 miles (483 km) from their homelands.

The Cheyenne wanted to trade furs for European knives, axes, needles, and guns. Their neighbors, the Sioux, the Cree, and the Assiniboine already had guns. These tribes used guns to drive the Cheyenne from their **ancestral** lands.

In 1804, the Lewis and Clark Expedition came upon the Cheyenne. The tribe had moved to the Black Hills of present-day South Dakota. Contact with the Americans soon became violent. The U.S. government wanted to make the Cheyenne lands part of America. They also wanted to force the Cheyenne onto **reservations**.

In 1861, Southern Cheyenne chief Black Kettle convinced the U.S. government to give the Cheyenne farmland. Black Kettle hoped the new land would bring peace to his people.

But in 1864, Colonel John M. Chivington led his U.S. troops on a surprise attack against Black Kettle's camp at Sand Creek, Colorado. Many Cheyenne, including women and children, were killed during the attack. It became known as the Sand Creek Massacre.

John M. Chivington

Black Kettle (circled)

At first, Chivington and his men were called heroes for their victory. Chivington left the army in 1865. But later that year, the U.S. government investigated the attack. Chivington was brought up on **court-martial** charges. Since he was no longer in the army, he could not be punished. Chivington was never charged with a crime. He died of cancer in 1894.

In 1868, Black Kettle's band was attacked along the Washita River in present-day Oklahoma by Lieutenant Colonel George Armstrong Custer and the U.S. Cavalry. The surprise attack led to more deaths of innocent people. Black Kettle also died in the attack.

George Armstrong Custer

Little Wolf & Dull Knife

Little Wolf and Dull Knife were two Old Man Chiefs of the Northern Cheyenne. The U.S. government had forced the Northern Cheyenne to the Southern Cheyenne Agency in present-day Oklahoma.

Living at the Agency was difficult. Many Cheyenne were sick and starving. Dull Knife and Little Wolf wanted to save their people. In 1878, they led an escape from the Agency.

Little Wolf led a band of healthy Cheyenne northward toward the homelands in Montana. Dull Knife led the sick people toward the Red Cloud Agency at Fort Robinson in present-day Nebraska. For four months, the Cheyenne avoided over 10,000 U.S. soldiers who were trying to capture them.

Little Wolf's band successfully returned to the northern homelands. The U.S. government gave them a **reservation** along the Tongue River. Dull Knife and his people made it safely to Fort Robinson. The Cheyenne honored both men as heroes.

Little Wolf (left) and Dull Knife

The Cheyenne Today

Today, the Cheyenne are working hard to preserve their **traditional** teachings, which they call the "Cheyenne Way." They still perform traditional religious ceremonies such as the Sun Dance, the Arrow Renewal, and the **Sacred** Buffalo Hat ceremonies.

In 1990, Congress passed the Native American Graves Protection and Repatriation Act (NAGPRA). The Act returns sacred items to Native Americans. Some of the items are necessary for ceremonies. The Act also returns burial items and remains that need to be reburied.

A cheyenne tipi

A cheyenne shield

28

Senator Ben Nighthorse Campbell is Northern Cheyenne. He was the first Native American elected to the U.S. **Senate** in 60 years.

Senator Campbell has fought hard for laws that are helpful to Native Americans. He helped create the National Museum of the American Indian within the Smithsonian Institution. He also helped to change the name of the Custer Battlefield Monument in Montana to the Little Bighorn Battlefield National Monument.

Senator Ben Nighthorse

Little Bighorn Battlefield National Monument

Cheyenne in traditional dress

29

The Southern Cheyenne live at the Cheyenne-Arapaho **reservation** in Concho, Oklahoma. More than 11,000 people live on its 70,000 acres (32,374 ha).

The Northern Cheyenne reservation is on the Tongue River in Montana. More than 6,000 people live on its 445,000 acres (180,082 ha).

A burial scaffold honors the Cheyenne killed at the Massacre of Washita.

Leaders and elders of the Northern Cheyenne Tribe at a ceremony for the 135th anniversary of the Sand Creek Massacre

The Washita Memorial dedication

Glossary

Algonquian - a family of Native American languages spoken from Labrador, Canada, to the Carolinas and westward into the Great Plains.

ancestor - a person from whom one is directly descended.

counting coup - a military game where Cheyenne warriors touched the enemy without killing him, then returned safely to camp.

court-martial - a military court that tries members of the armed forces for offenses against military law.

cradleboard - a decorated flat board with a wooden band at the top that protects the baby's head.

Erect Horns - a Cheyenne leader who went to a sacred mountain to seek spiritual guidance and end a famine.

insulate - to keep something from losing heat by lining it with a material.

legend - a story handed down from the past, which many people have believed.

myth - a legend or story that tries to explain nature.

nomads - people who have no permanent home but move season by season looking for food, water, and grazing land.

prophet - a person who tells what will happen.

raid - a sudden attack.

reservation - a piece of land set aside by the U.S. government to be lived on only by a Native American tribe.

sacred - spiritual or religious.

Senate - the upper and smaller part of the U.S. Congress.

supernatural - above or beyond the forces or laws of nature.

talons - claws from a bird of prey, such as an eagle or a hawk.

tan - to make a hide into leather by soaking in a special liquid.

tradition - the handing down of beliefs, customs, and stories from parents to children.

travois - a simple vehicle used by the Cheyenne to move goods and people. A travois was made with two long tipi poles tied together to form a big triangle. Toward the bottom of the triangle, shorter poles were tied onto the tipi poles. The shorter poles formed a platform that carried food, children, and the elderly.

vision quest - a journey to witness the mystical or supernatural.

Web Sites

For general information about the Cheyenne, visit the Smithsonian's Web site:
http://www.si.edu/organiza/museums/amerind/abmus/index.htm

Or visit the official Cheyenne Web sites:
• Northern Cheyenne: **http://tlc.wtp.net/northern.htm**
• Southern Cheyenne: **http://www.cheyenne-arapaho.nsn.us/culture/culture.htm**

For info about the Cheyenne language, visit **http://listen.to/cheyenne.pictures**

These sites are subject to change. Go to your favorite search engine and type in "Cheyenne" for more sites.

Index